Edited by Vic Parker
Designed by Janet Jamieson

Published by Hodder Children's Books 1998

10 9 8 7 6 5 4 3 2 1

ISBN 0340 71354 2

Printed and bound in Great Britain by
the Guernsey Press Co. Ltd, Channel Isles

Hodder Children's Books
A division of Hodder Headline plc
338 Euston Road
London NW1 3BH

CHOOSE YOUR SUPERHERO

poems by
Norman Silver

illustrations by
Russell Ayto

*Hodder
Children's
Books*

a division of Hodder Headline plc

Contents

Day of Doom: *Part 1*

Mutations

It's unbelievable! Carol, my best friend,
is growing talons! She scratches at my eyes
and rips my clothes! Long fangs descend
from her mouth and to everyone's surprise

she becomes the bloodsucking Vampirelle.
Wearing a spooky black mask and cloak,
she turns nasty, lets out a fearsome yell
and, in front of the whole class, no joke,

bites Miss Baker savagely on her pale
neck. Later in the gym, Sue Price grows
wings and flies around the hall with a trail
of fire and smoke gushing from her toes

She calls herself Flame and sets the place
alight before zooming off to perpetrate
other crimes! Next it's the turn of babyface
Mark Yan, a dozy lad, who begins to mutate,

during history, to the size of a juggernaut!
This oaf who was once so quiet and serene
now stomps on kids who are weak and short
while his skin turns hairy and bright green!

I avoid being squelched by Goliathon's shoes
and run for my life, but as I get to the door
of the headmaster, I see a terrible ooze
of blood streaming out onto the lobby floor.

I must get away, I think, but with a hiss
he emerges and I'm transfixed by the sight!
A poisonous, scaly serpent, with endless
coils, slithers towards me. I nearly die of fright

as the Cobraman approaches, but at the last
moment, my feet move and I'm out of there!
I want to escape from this nightmare as fast
as possible, but monsters are everywhere!

I run to the caretaker for help, but that kind
old man has become the Gorgon, his room
littered with skeletons and bones. I must find
someone to save us from this impending doom!

. . . continued on page 41 . . .

A Card for Mother's Day

Cuddlier than a nettle,
kinder than a great white shark,
jollier than a graveyard
at midnight in the dark,

calmer than a thunderstorm,
neater than sloshy mud,
more elegant than a hippo
or a cow that's chewing cud,

lovelier than a potato,
gentler than an avalanche,
more charming than a squawking crow
squatting on its branch,

livelier than a bathroom sponge,
warmer than Arctic Ice,
more generous than a teaspoon
with a single grain of rice,

softer than a ball and chain,
wiser than a wooden plank,
because today is Mother's Day
it's you I have to thank

for everything you've done for me,
for keeping me in your clutch,
you're sweeter than lime pickle
and I love you very much.

Hard

Jason beats up kids,
  he's hard.
Rants and rages
when he's jarred.

Burps and swears and spits,
  he's hard.
Cruel to creatures,
no regard.

Jason throws his weight,
  he's hard.
He's the top dog
in the yard.

Clubs and cafés know
  he's hard.
He's been expelled
and he's been barred.

Jason has no friends,
   he's hard.
Often injured,
badly scarred.

Never shows his pain,
   he's hard.
Always has to be
on guard.

Always has to be
on guard,
never shows his pain,
   he's hard.

The Eczema Tribe

Openly we dwell
among the nations,
splendid as scarlet
lizards on stone walls,
our scaly skins
an armour against
the smooth clans.

We worship the flames
of the itching sun
which has marked us
for a life of ritual
painting on of creams
or ceremonial dips
in mineral baths.

The swamp crocodile
is our totem, our
primeval strength.
We go into battle
like tattooed warriors
against the old enemy
who makes us scratch.

We are the bandage
tribe, the mitten
and stocking tribe.
Awesome as dragons
on volcanic islands
we greet you
with fiery embrace.

Clouds

Clouds often stampede across the sky
as if they were in a desperate rush
to reach the dark side of the world.
But on lazy days they glide like goldfish
through the spaces of their enormous pond.

Sometimes they are as colourful as beads
hanging around the graceful neck
of evening. At other times
as ominous as ghosts, treading
heavily on our finicky worlds.

Isn't it wonderful that they roam freely
as antelopes once did on the great plains
of Africa and that no-one owns them?
From nowhere they come, with their bulk
of smoky vapours, these soft dragons,

magically shape-changing
or disappearing without trace
before our unbelieving eyes.
And don't they rage when they get
in a black mood, spitting down rain

on whoever happens to be below,
hurling live zigzags of lightning
at spires and towers and trees!
Afterwards they'll be innocent
as a flock of grazing sheep.

Word Game

Think of
a word. Multiply it
by its meaning. Subtract
the shortest syllable. Reverse
the order of the remaining letters. Add
the first noun that comes to mind. Substitute
vowels for any two consonants. Divide
by its nearest synonym. Write
down your result. Check
the spelling. Answer:
snorkel.

Box of Dreams

Inside my box of dreams is a pack
   of winged unicorns
which gallop me to the end of time.
   On their flanks
are painted the sun and moon
   and their tails
are galaxies of blazing stars.
   Oh, sometimes
it's magnificent to leap beyond
   the humdrum
on a creature made of light.

Inside my box of dreams grow trees
   with roots
in the resting places of our ancestors
   and branches
fruiting in the thunderous skies.
   Birds with human
faces perch among the topaz leaves:
   I recognise
you all, my valiant beautiful brothers,
   my charming sisters,
my father and mother of all things.

Inside my box of dreams are enemies
    too malignant
to face during the waking hours:
    the nameless
beasts with horns and deadened eyes
    who gorge on
the minutes and seconds of my life.
    But see them scatter
when I raise my sword of fire:
    fear shows
in their yellow eyes as they melt.

Inside my box of dreams I am
    as ancient
as the wishbone of a dinosaur
    and as newborn
as this moment hatched from breath.
    I am stripped
of the clothes I usually hide in
    and the skin
of words I wrap around my heart.
    How marvellous
sometimes to be spirited away.

One Way Trip
to Lemming Heaven

My dear rodents,
in your hour of need
I am here to deliver you
from your own obedience.

When you would so willingly
leap off the edge towards death
I will show you a path of survival.

Where there is rock
   I will make you diggers.
Where the earth is deep
   I will make you miners.
Where there is danger
   I will make you blockers of the road.
Where there is void
   I will make you builders of bridges.
Where there is plummeting
   I will make you floaters.

My brave ones,
I am here to guide you
beyond the fiery gate.
If not all of you, then
at least a high percentage.
The few who will be exploded
en route will be sacrificed
for the majority.

I will extricate you from traps,
solve the puzzles of existence
before your time expires.

So, dear lemmings,
march to your brief music
with uniform submission.
But remember –
whether it be
  fun,
    tricky,
      taxing
        or mayhem,
your destiny is in my hands.

Remember, Remember

This November Dad didn't even buy us sparklers
but took us instead to the display in the park

where thousands of pounds of fireworks
were reduced to smoke and ashes in a thirty minute

non-stop frenzy by the Albion Pyrotechnic Company.
Volleys of rockets whizzed into the frozen night

and lit up the dark with dazzling explosions
of glitzy sparks and multi-coloured rain.

The bangers were so thunderous the ground shook.
It sounded like a city being blitzed.

The Catherine wheels seemed to spin forever
like galaxies whirling through outer space.

Electric waterfalls leaped off imaginary cliffs
and volcanoes erupted with bursts of golden lava.

My little brother cried and covered his ears
but I loved every moment except the last,

when three lads aimed their bottle at the crowd,
and their fizzy rocket struck my dad near the left eye.

We spent the rest of the evening in Casualty
where Dad was treated for burns and bruising.

He was in agony and had to wear a bandage
but grateful that his eyesight wasn't damaged.

Old Folks

Me grandma smell of powder,
me grandpa stubble chin.
She pray to God for mercy,
he prefer to sin.

Me grandma do de cooking,
me grandpa do de pools.
She strict on law and order,
he got to break de rules.

Me grandma plump and podgy,
me grandpa skin and bone.
She full of chitter-chatter,
he quiet and alone.

Me grandma always smiling,
me grandpa always frown.
She clothes all fresh and frilly,
he wear hand-me-down.

Me grandma sweet as heaven,
me grandpa gruff as hell.
She love me grandpa tenderly,
he soft on her as well.

And Now for Something Completely Different

A visitor needing the bathroom
was already enthroned
when she caught sight of Monty
and almost passed out.

Those who were still spooning
their iced desserts
discovered her beside the loo
with knickers in a twist.

She was pointing – but they knew
they'd not mentioned
Monty to her: soaking his coils
after a tiring day.

Evan bought the snake when young
to his mother's horror
and bred live mice in the garage
to feed him on.

At first, boy and python bathed
together, the reptile
mesmerised by steam, only his head
above the water-line.

But now at three and a half metres
Monty uses the tub alone
and his diet is supplemented
with deep-frozen rats.

Mostly he hangs out in Evan's room;
except on winter nights
he joins the family in the lounge
around the electric fire.

He doesn't like to be told off
for going too close.
If moved, he'll slither back
to the tropical heat.

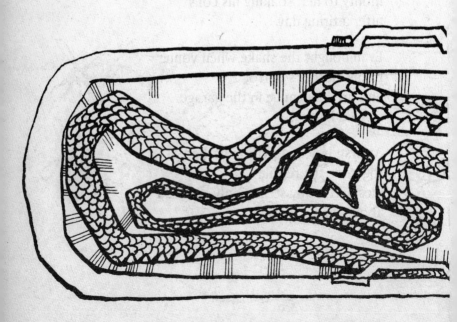

And Mother adores him, forgetting –
on purpose? – to tell guests
about her reticulated friend.
Often she'll step outside

garlanded with python, tickling
him under the chin.
Neighbours back off, gossip about
the cult she's got involved in.

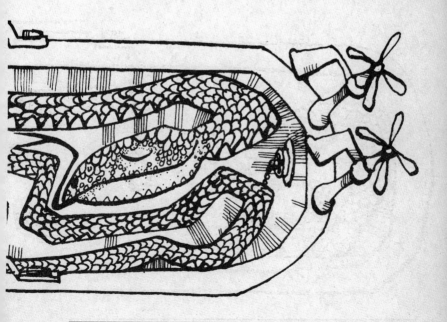

Elements

Earth, fire, water, air,
joy, anger, hope, despair.

Fire, water, air, earth,
age, youth, death, birth.

Water, air, earth, fire,
love, envy, hate, desire.

Air, earth, fire, water,
father, mother, son and daughter.

Music

Music is the dripping of sound
    into a pool of silence.
Or the wakening of birds
    after a frosty winter.

Music is a photograph
    of the wind's howl.
Or the healing ointment
    found in moonlight.

Music is the shape of your fear
    and its slaying.
Or a carpet woven
    of joy and melancholy.

Music is the galloping
    of untamed horses.
Or a ride on the big-wheel
    with legs dangling.

Music is the stutter of carriages
    on a railway track.
Or your mother's voice before
    you understood words.

Surface

The pond is wet
and wrapped in a sheet

of gold spangles. Water-boat-
men float

upside down at
the surface lying in wait

for a bite
of tadpole or baby trout.

The girl, whose feet
each wear an anklet

of ripples, hunts crested newt
with a stocking-net.

Pondskaters dart
across the water's delicate

skin. Where the bulrushes meet
their reflections, a coot

swims out
over a silhouette

of willows. The crowfoot,
with its root

in mud, presents its white
blossoms to the light.

Blue damselflies flit
and mirror their sunlit

wings. With beak like a bayonet
a kingfisher stabs the taut

surface of the pool and a fat
stickleback is caught.

Buried Treasure

The house Dan moved to didn't have a garden.
Just some flowerbeds overgrown with cow
    parsley and nettles.
His step-dad, Reggie, asked him to help dig
the ground, but Dan said: 'Why should I? I liked
    the old place better.'

So Reggie started digging while Dan sulked
in his lonely new room. Through the window
    he could see Reggie's back.
It was cold out there, the tail-end of winter
or beginning of spring. Mum brought Dan soup
    to warm up his thoughts.

Reggie turned over the soil with his spade.
He took off his anorak and rolled his sleeves.
    Dan could see his tattoo,
which said: 'Jenny, love you forever', in a red
heart surrounded with roses. Dan's mother's name
    was not Jennifer.

Suddenly the iron blade struck something solid.
Reggie bent and searched the soil with his hands.
    He found the hard lump.
He brushed the dirt off with his shirt-sleeve
then turned and held it towards the house so Dan
    could see what it was.

'What is it?' Dan asked. Reggie offered it to him
through the open window. It was a pure pink rock
   as large as his fist.
'I think that's quartz,' he said, 'rose quartz.
I don't know why it's buried in this patch,
   but isn't it spectacular?

Here, you can have it.' Dan scrubbed off the dirt
with an old toothbrush, washed the rose quartz,
   dried it with a towel.
It was almost shiny but with no sharp edges.
And pink as a heavy lump of sugar-candy.
   Dan put it on his table.

It looked mysterious. Not long after, he heard
the sounds of another lucky strike. The rock
   was almost transparent
with just a hint of rainbow colours. Reggie
passed it to Dan. 'This is interesting,' he said.
   Looks to me like rock-crystal.'

Dan washed it and put it with the rose quartz,
then slipped on a jumper to go outside and help.
   He found a garden fork
and started digging alongside his step-dad.
They reached the far end of the messy rectangle
   before they struck again.

The prongs of Dan's fork hit something hard.
Excitedly he dug out his piece of treasure.
  It was dirty and ugly.
Dan thought it was just a piece of rubbish
but Reggie said: 'Looks like you found a beauty.'
  'What is it?' Dan asked.

Reggie's thumbs worked loose the clods of earth
which clung to it and Dan could see transparent
  purple crystal shapes
sparkling in a stone that from the outside
looked like an ugly and broken cannon-ball.
  'It's a purple amethyst,'

Reggie announced. They showed the three
precious stones to Mum who held each of them
    up to the sunlight.
'What good fortune,' she said, 'to uncover
such exquisite stones in a garden that's been
    neglected for years.'

Since then Dan and Reggie have turned over
all the flowerbeds and found nothing else.
    But it's been worthwhile.
The roses, marigolds and irises are flourishing,
while Dan's gems speak brightly to him
    of ancient earth magic.

Glass Boy

Jonathon Brittle
moulded of glass,
is fragile and nervous
of kids in class.

If ever they stone him
or push him around,
he'll surely shatter
to bits on the ground.

He won't go outdoors,
he can't jump or run.
He never plays sports
or has much fun.

Every thought in his head
is always on view.
It must be distressing
to be seen through.

He longs for a buddy
with time to spare.
But the sign on his back reads:
HANDLE WITH CARE.

Like a delicate crystal
he knows that he'd crack
if ever he came under
serious attack.

The hammer lads tease him –
that's not fair –
to bully a kid
with glass face and hair!

Jonathon Brittle,
I'd help if I could –
if you were a stone boy
or carved of wood.

But you're so transparent
I can see your soul.
And if I break you
who'll make you whole?

My House

has two windows
   for me to spy on the ample world
   of skyscrapers, wasps and hurricanes;

has a thatched roof
   which protects me from rain and bird-droppings
   but where diverse creatures lay their eggs;

has thin walls
   on which the winds dance and the sun plays hot;

has a front door
   for me to take in the earth's fruit
   or pass coded messages to the outside world;

has a chimney
   through which precious air ebbs and flows;

has two aerials
   for me to tune in to the hubbub of neighbours
   and the music of lawn-mowers, xylophones or geese;

has an attic
   where photographs of the past are hung
   and pictures of the future painted.

Day of Doom: *Part 2*

The Z-Force

... continued from page 8 ...

The Story So Far ...

The situation at school has become dire
with everyone mutating over the past weeks.
Every kid has become an ogre or a vampire
and the staff have turned into killer freaks.

Now Read On ...

Here comes the dinner lady, Mrs Weir.
At least she hasn't changed her shape.
Or has she? As soon as she gets near
I can see she's wearing a leopardskin cape.

In fact, she has spots around her eyes
and whiskered cheeks. 'Mrs Weir, have you
also transformed?' I ask. 'Yes, 'she replies,
'I am the Leopard Lady. Someone has to do

something about this scandalous outbreak.'
She looks like she's entering a fancy dress
competition but at least she's prepared to take
action. 'Well,' she says, 'you're done for, unless

you join my Z-Force to fight the Dark Lord.'
'What's going on?' I ask. 'Don't you know,'
the Leopard Lady says, 'that the school Board
was bought out and taken over some time ago

by the foul and dastardly Lord Quox. Even now
he's in his Castle concocting wicked schemes
to control the minds of pupils and staff. How?
He does it by aiming psychotronic laser beams

at the pineal gland deep within our brain.
So if I was you, girl, I'd change personality
this minute, before Quox drives you insane.
Which superhero would you like to be?'

I hear an urgency in the Leopard Lady's voice.
But what if she's an agent working for Quox?
On the other hand, I don't have much choice.
So I say 'The Phantom' and she opens this box

and tells me to select an outfit. Of course
I go for the slinky body-suit. I slip into the gear
and as I clasp the buckle an invisible force
surges up my spine, dispelling all fear.

. . . continued on page 71 . . .

Mixed Up

When sun sets like jelly I eat it,
when day breaks I mend it with glue,
when night falls I help it get back on its feet –
   it's still got the night-shift to do.

When baths run I sprint off to catch them,
when clocks strike I never hit back,
when locks jam I keep them in neat-labelled jars –
   I pick them when I need a snack.

When sides split I stitch them with cotton,
when truth hurts I plaster the pain,
when looks kill I die and I bury myself
   till I'm ready to face life again.

A Time of Illness

Your mum bought a giant jigsaw puzzle which you
laid out on the flat arena of a tray: corner pieces,
straight edges, sky blues, trees, roof tiles, flowers.

Mornings melted into afternoon and still the picture
never completed itself, though slowly getting there,
the doctor said, packing away his stethoscope.

She phoned from work, your mum, each coffee break,
just a brief call to say *Hello, my sweet, how are you?*
One day she came home with a portable TV.

The soap stars kept you company, their theme tunes
marking the progression of life in Somewhere Street
as blood-feuds erupted, causing mayhem for a week.

You learned who your friends were: Dilena brought
a porcelain pig because she knew you loved them.
Jess swopped you a magazine each time she came.

Derek slipped in and out the house like a foreign spy.
He never shut up, with his bottomless bag of gossip:
who was doing what, who with, and where and when.

Your dad held your hand each evening when he got in
from the office, always with a joke, his eyes, like jugs
pouring strength into you, if only it worked like that.

And dear Aunt Trish spent every morning at the house:
cooking your soups and stews, then producing a pack
of cards to gamble with you till she went broke.

Daylight Robbery

Shopkeeper, are you awake
or are you only pretending
to sell sweets and chocolates?

Are those beady eyes shut
or is there enough of a slit
to detect nicking fingers?

Don't worry, I'm not one
of those crazy kids
with a Kalashnikov rifle

who'd blow your brains out
if you didn't hand over
a couple of Bounty Bars.

Honestly, I'm not a thug.
In my pocket are jangling coins
to pay for what I want.

Shopkeeper, wake yourself up!
I could walk out with half
your stock of Smarties.

Don't you know the world
is a savage place these days?
You have to keep an eye on it.

Oh, alright then, if you don't
want to take my money, you've
only got yourself to blame.

The King of Sutton Hoo

Who sails the ship at Sutton Hoo
and which way is it heading?
A royal sleep prepared for you
but dark earth for your bedding.

Forty coins to pay your crew
but nobody is rowing.
Who'll steer the ship from Sutton Hoo
when the River Deben's flowing?

A broad shield, a sword once true,
an iron helmet rusting.
Who'll save the King of Sutton Hoo
when wild storms come gusting?

Hear the harp at Sutton Hoo,
its silent music ringing!
Where are the minstrels you once knew
that filled your halls with singing?

Inlaid jewels, red and blue –
golden buckles shining.
Who carved the knots at Sutton Hoo
with arms and tails entwining?

A pagan lord and convert too –
was Raedwald's standard flying
when you were laid in Sutton Hoo,
High King of England dying?

Prehistoric Pen-pal

It's the Ice Age and he's glad to be there!
The woolly mammoths have trudged
from France to England across the green valley

that will one day be the Channel.
Last week he saw a herd of shaggy mothers
with their offspring lumbering through Piccadilly

with their domed skulls and twisting tusks.
And from a vantage point on Hampstead Heath
he witnessed two irate and trumpeting bulls

challenge each other to an awesome duel.
One crushed the shoulder of his rival.
It didn't take long for the hyenas to sniff out

the carcass and tuck into the flesh.
After the scavengers finished their bloody meal
he managed to strip good hunks of meat

to haul back to his people sheltering in their cave.
Later, when the bones were dry,
he played them like a drum or xylophone.

He's keen on music and enjoys dancing
when he gets a break from Stone Age chores.
But life in Britain will never be the same

now the weather is warming up: it's been eons
since ice reached as far south as Ilford.
He's sad to hear the mammoths won't survive.

Winter Olympics

This year we were prepared: as soon
as the snow thickened we fetched out
our plastic toboggans, each
with handles for breaking and steering.

We plodded across the donkey track:
our footprints were the first and deep
as buckets until we got nearer
and sloshed along with the crowd.

It was the field where we photographed
the foal last summer: now video cameras
were rolling and we all would soon star
in someone or other's home movie.

Parents chattered on the hill-crest:
neighbours who hadn't spoken for years
were suddenly pleased to meet each other
and huddle together against the cold.

Flasks of tea released their genies
in a swirl of steam: every adult's wish
was a cup of something hot and a biscuit
handed round from mitten to glove.

The kids were in a different groove:
over and over we attacked the slope,
feetfirst, headfirst, three on a sled,
criss-crossing the pasture with screams.

A ramp was built from packed snow
near the bottom where the river froze
in its bed: after a few trial runs
we soon learnt how to defy gravity.

We all bulleted down the hill,
flew over the ramp, jolted to a stop
a hair's breadth from the wire fence
with its deadly armoury of barbs.

One parent struggling against getting old
tried all morning to steer his toboggan
over the ramp: tugging the handles,
he zigged and zagged out of control.

Finally he achieved it, soaring
majestically upwards into the brisk sky.
It was such an embarrassing display!
And the landing hurt my dad's back.

Haik-Haik-Haik

Mallards laughing in
the reeds: a duckling must have
quacked a little joke.

Intermission

This is half-time
when you can leave your seats
to go buy candyfloss or sweets.

A brief interval
to ponder what has gone before
or anticipate the thrills in store.

Now is the moment
to chat to friends or get to know
the bloke sitting in the next row.

And if you're bursting
with another hour to sit through
an opportunity to use the loo.

Phone Lines

1.

Awaken from your slumber!
No time now for long distance dreaming
on your comfortable settee.

2.

His bell rings equally for all:
I could never have guessed
it was the Prince of Darkness calling.

3.

O phone!
Go off and bring me the voice of my grandmother!

4.

Throughout the hot season
quick-legged ants in single file
trooped up and down the cord
each bearing a back-pack.

5.

Behold the aperture
through which my thousand arms
embrace family and friends!

6.

Grey cat, curled up
always in the same place,
purrs
when you press her against your face.

7.

Lightning!
You make me leap
out of my bubble bath.

8.

If you are not silent
I will take you off the hook
and leave you numb all day!

Mirror Image

Sometimes I look in the mirror
and wonder who looks back.
I stare at his eyes and all I get
for an answer are two black dots.

Is that myself I'm seeing there
or a thin ghost copying my actions
but reversing them left to right
for reasons of his own?

It feels uncomfortable standing
face to face with an alien
who is able to hold my gaze
exactly as long as I hold his.

To break the spell I wink at him
and, true to form, he winks back
as we leave in opposite directions
to continue our separate lives.

Perhaps in the years ahead
we can become acquainted,
gently discover who is really
looking out through these eyes.

Picturama!

Gilli's beddy is pasted with loadsa
photies and pics of sizzlin' chappies:
I mean four walls plus on the ceiling!

The parents find it, to say the least,
spewgusting, but to us it's a fabuloso
patchwork of hunkmungousness.

Babelicious filmsters,
      coolmundo glamourlads,
            hot-rockin' songsters,

bicep-tastic gladiators,
      phwoarrsome models
            high-scorin' footie stars.

Big bro' thinks it's well time for Gilli
to land a real-live boyfy, but she is tres
content at the mo', ta very much,

with her gallery of glistening bods.
We've been bezzy mates, Gilli and me,
since we were wee popsicles, and I know

she's a chickstrel with a mind of her own.
When Mr Spesh comes along she'll be
ready and waiting. So, purlease, leave out

the slagging sesh and pass the blue-tac!
We've got some serious decorating to do!
Gilli's room is our private swoonland,

our groovacious island in the boring
expanse of nothing-ever-happensness
where we keep company with celebs

and eyeball the array of gorge blokeys
staring back at us. Doncha know,
we could fall in lurve with all of 'em!

And if sometimes we invite friends
around for a natter and a goss, and if
sometimes we get a bit too rowdious,

playing our fave record of the week
repeatedly at mega-decibel volumes
while wagglin' our botties at the world,

fret not! We are the luvliest ladettes
that ever were and those snootsome
neighbs should mind their own biz!

Life Story

At the age of ninety, Nan
is writing her autobiography,
lavish with details of life
as it used to be:

how the folk in her village
starved and suffered
from rickets during
the years of unemployment;

how father worked the steam-
driven threshing machine;
how mother was stricken
with rheumatoid arthritis

and permanently bed-ridden
at the age of fifty;
how the first wireless
was set up in mother's bedroom –

the accumulator, the horn,
the big square box,
the aerial in the tree –
and the thrill of the boat race;

how she heard an inner voice
announce that one day
she would own the house
at the end of the road;

how the new school-teacher
told her to *use her brain.*
'What is a brain?' she asked
her father who was out

the back skinning a rabbit.
Her father obligingly
split open the rabbit's skull
and showed young Grace.

'No,' she cried, 'I don't
have anything like that
horrible mess inside me!'
Later she went to sit

in the branches of her tree,
the one called 'Fangus'
grown from a walking-stick
her father had planted.

In that place of contemplation
she asked her god
to reveal what her brain was
and how she could use it.

The answer came later
in the sand when her finger drew
patterns: a room with numerous
cupboards and shelves.

Now at ninety she says
it's easy to write her story.
All she has to do is enter
that dusty vault, fetch down

the ordered contents
and commit them to the page
before the cataracts seal
her eyes against the light.

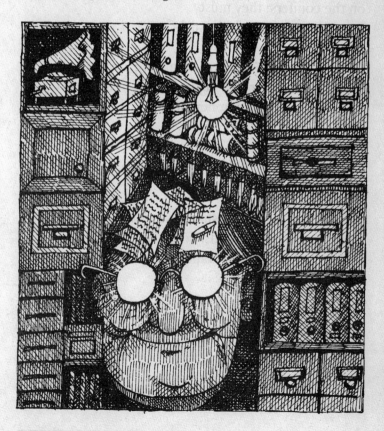

Diadem Spiders

Sun crouching behind
the comfrey, webs newly spun:
visitors welcome.

> Trembling livewires of
> fairy lights: radiating
> avenues of dew.

Silver necklaces
on the conifers: they must
have danced through the night.

> Eight legs balancing
> on the tightrope between shed
> and honeysuckle.

If only we'd heard
the hum of those spinnerets
and the twang of silk!

> When she was human
> the gods were jealous of her
> woven tapestries.

Boy in a Crash Helmet

Andrew Hale,
soft as a snail,
enemies surround him.
He can't say
why he won't play
or why his mother's bound him.

Andrew Hale,
fierce and frail,
fists that punch and pound him.
He's never known
that they're his own
that damage and dumbfound him.

Andrew Hale,
arms that flail,
human words astound him.
Though he may try,
he can't reply
to the aliens around him.

Flowerfall

The day it rained flowers
Mrs Doyle had just pegged up her kimono.
'It's going to ruin my washing,' she said
feeling the first drops of gladioli on her skin.

Next door, the newly-wed
phoned relatives in the Punjab to inform them
how splendid an English summer was after all.
'Oh it's pretty. London is so pink and purple.'

The TV weatherman used maps
to show how Yorkshire had received the worst
of the fuschias and Cornwall was blanketed
with a patchwork of orchids and tiger-lilies.

He apologised for failing
to predict the gale force hollyhocks
which took the roofs off in the hills of Wales.
'According to the Met Office,' he explained,

'this shouldn't be happening.'
But a drizzle of nasturtiums in the afternoon
was followed by a deluge of forget-me-nots
and the motorways had to be sealed off.

There were some casualties:
a bridegroom on the way to his wedding
was lost in a drift of marigolds and geraniums
while a policeman allergic to petunias

was rushed to Intensive Care.
On a brighter note a woman who attempted
suicide from the sixteenth floor of a city bank
landed on a soft mattress of chrysanthemums.

Flowers fell for forty days
and forty nights: visionaries constructed arks
to save themselves from death by petals.
But as suddenly as it started, it stopped,

with just a hint of rainbow.
Within a week the debris biodegraded
and newspapers turned their headlines
to the phenomenon of watery rain

which threatened October.
Within a month scientists produced proof
that flowers can't grow in the atmosphere
and therefore none had dropped from the sky.

Within a year nobody
would confess to the miraculous downpour
except for a young girl who had pressed
pansies between the pages of her diary.

Day of Doom: *Part 3*

Inside Quox Castle

. . . continued from page 42 . . .

The Story So Far . . .

I have become the fearless Phantom who'll
do anything to help the Leopard Lady fight
against Quox, before he destroys our school.
We must save staff and pupils from their plight!

Now Read On . . .

'Let's go,' the Leopard Lady says, and strange
as it seems, we're soon flying out of town.
We whiz across a wild ocean, beyond a range
of snowy mountains and finally come down

on a parapet in Quox Castle. 'Hold your breath!'
the Leopard Lady cautions me. 'If we're caught,
he'll make sure we have a slow and painful death.'
I'm balancing on this ledge, thinking I ought

never have got myself into this, but she breaks
a window and we enter. I'm sure we were seen
by guards, but that's just one of our small mistakes.
Inside Quox's laboratory, on a computer screen

I see a model of our school and a detailed list
of each and every person who's been morphed.
I look for my name but suddenly, with a twist
of a key, in come two Wormguards, dwarfed

by the hideous figure of Lord Quox. 'How sweet
of you, Leopard Lady, to visit me!' he howls.
'My devastating Phantom, at last we meet!'
I quiver and shake, but Leopard Lady growls:

'Your days are numbered, Quox! It is decreed
that your reign of terror will be brought to an end
by the Phantom with her lightning speed
reflexes and body shields. You can't defend

your kingdom from inevitable collapse.'
'That's what you think,' Quox says, as he flicks
a switch. A circle of fiery gamma-light traps
the Leopard Lady. Another series of clicks

and I too am surrounded by deadly laser rays.
Suddenly I hear myself say: 'Do you really believe
your little tricks can stop me?' As if in a daze
I lift both arms. My sizzling fingers cleave

the barriers of light and I step out unharmed.
Now I know what to do: smash the activator cells
and detach the control panel. Quox is alarmed!
'Don't let her near the machine! Kill her!' he yells.

. . . continued on page 94 . . .

My Grandfather

Who told me the story
  of the world's beginning?
Grandfather.

Who gave me the book
  with the skeleton pictures?
Grandfather.

Who showed me the gun-wound
  on his old shin-bone?
Grandfather.

Who taught me to speak
  the words of the old language?
Grandfather.

Who made me walk tall
  in the city of exile?
Grandfather.

Who's waiting for the flying ship
  to swoop him home?
Grandfather.

On First Looking into Tolkien's *Lord of the Rings*

How mind-boggling to be transported by black
runes on a white page from Bag-End, Hobbiton
in the Shire to the accursed Gate of Morannon
in the Land of Mordor, where the shadows lie.

How breath-taking to join Frodo, Gandalf
and the rest of the Company on their perilous
travels over the Misty Mountains in a quest
to unmake the One Ring of the Dark Lord.

How hair-raising to journey beyond the valley
of Rivendell and pass beneath mountains
through the vast and gloomy Mines of Moria
where priceless Mithril was dug by dwarves.

How gut-wrenching to be at the narrow bridge
of Khazad-dum where the Balrog and Gandalf
plunge into the abyss – and to witness the death
of Boromir and the breaking of the Fellowship.

How nail-biting to cross the Plains of Rohan
into Gondor heading towards seven-levelled
Minas Tirith, Tower of the Sun and the ghastly
city of Minas Morgul, Tower of the Moon.

How blood-curdling to be confronted by hordes
of Sauron's orcs and Nazgul on winged beasts
led by the terrifying Witch-king of Angmar
during the Battle of the Pelennor Fields.

How spine-tingling to climb the fire-belching
summit of Orodruin, Mountain of Doom,
where the wretched Gollum meets his end
and the precious Ring is finally destroyed.

How heart-warming to see Gandalf on Gwaihir,
Lord of the Eagles, rescuing Sam and Frodo
from the Land of Darkness – and to celebrate
the rightful crowning of Aragorn the King.

Travellers

One Friday they appeared at school
out of nowhere: John, Brendan, Paul,

Billy, the littlest one with his blonde hair
over his eyes like curtains, Cahill, Clare,

Mary, with freckles, and James, so strong
he beat everyone at arm-wrestling.

They had come to live for part of the summer
on the wasteland behind the old cinema.

They hung their washing out on lines
between their long white caravans

and one night three of their men sat
around a fire having a chat:

that's what I saw when I went past.
At assembly the vicar said: 'A guest

is someone you should welcome
into your town and into your home

so let's say hello to our new friends.'
We all clapped hands.

Little Billy, the smallest in the hall,
stood up and said: 'I'm glad to meet you's all.'

During breaks we followed them
and if they wanted to play a game

we let them join in. It all went well
until Mary was hit in the face by a ball

and wow, did James go mad!
He thumped the boy who kicked it and said:

'Don't you ever hurt my cousin again!'
After a week we all got on

and when Brendan was put into my class
he showed me how to draw a horse

cantering over the wild moors.
And he made me speak up because his ears

were deaf. We worked together
on Vikings and he told me his father

was good with cement and bricks.
I told him mine worked down the docks.

On the way home I let him ride my bike
and he asked if I would like

to come round to meet his dog one day.
I didn't know what my mum would say.

But next morning he was gone.
And so was little Billy, Cahill, John,

Clare and freckled Mary, Paul and James.
No-one answered to their names

at registration, and it was only after lunch
that I heard about the wild bunch

of men who had attacked the caravan site
in the middle of the night.

The travellers were forced to leave the county,
escorted by the police for their own safety.

Our class wrote Brendan a note,
which we don't know if he ever got,

in which we said we were sorry
that he'd had to leave in such a hurry.

Adults

They often look so mean and miserable
with their cross faces and briefcases.

During the week they long for the weekend
but even when work's done they don't have fun.

When they exercise it seems to be agony
in those jogging boots and track-suits.

They've forgotten what it's like to wake up eager
for endless hours of eye-spying and kite-flying.

Now all they ever do is talk to each other
on mobile-phones about home-loans.

And wait for the future to relax
with pipe dreams and pension schemes.

Ruby and Her Dad

Behind the piano late one summer morning
Dad came across young Ruby playing truant.
He said: 'Come on, my love, you've had a warning.
You know you made a promise that you wouldn't.

The head's already phoned me to enquire
why you've missed another day of schooling.
She says the consequences will be dire
if you don't keep your word to quit this fooling.'

Ruby sulked and eyed him through her glasses:
the little dear was nearly twelve years old.
'I don't enjoy those stupid, boring classes
where every fact is neatly pigeonholed.'

Before he could reply she started playing
a jazzy blues she'd worked out on her own.
How could Dad scold the child for not obeying –
when he was home to play his saxophone?

The Magician

Watch carefully!
I wrap the caterpillar
in a silk cocoon.
(See, it can't get out.)
I snap my fingers,
utter a magic spell
and behold!
A butterfly.

Next I place a cow
in a field of green grass.
I wave my wand over it
and hey presto!
White milk.

Finally, an acorn.
Please pass it
among yourselves.
Check that it has
no secret compartments.
Now I bury it in earth
and sprinkle it with rain.
Abra cadabra!
A mighty oak.

Thank you
for your applause.

On the Streets

Excuse me, missus, give us a fag.
I'm dying for a drag.

No way, girl, you're too young to smoke.

Come on, missus, give us a quid.
You can see I'm addicted.

No way, girl, you're too young to be taking drugs.

Missus, my baby needs something to eat.
It's cold on the street.

No way, girl, you're too young to have given birth.

Please, missus, take me home.
I'm housetrained and I need a mum.

No way, girl, you're too old.

Waterclock

From the tap
first one
pear-drop

then another
precisely
drips

streams
to the plughole
blows

a bubble
in the centre
of its grid

then plips.

Dear Monica

Help me please! I feel so guilty.
Last week I was angry with my friend.
I lied about her and she was expelled.
I don't want our relationship to end.

I become nervous when I talk to boys:
I know that my face turns bright red
and I can't think of anything interesting
to say. Sometimes I wish I was dead.

Am I a psychopath? I regularly
take money from my mother's purse.
She hasn't noticed yet but she will
if my stealing habits get any worse.

I have unattractive knobbly knees
which show if I wear short skirts.
I think boys laugh at my appearance:
you don't know how much this hurts.

I'm a one-off, I'm a misfit.
You should see the colour of my skin.
I feel like I come from another planet.
Wherever I go I don't fit in.

I always find hairs on my clothes
and little scraggly bits of fluff.
You must tell me: is this common
or am I suffering from dandruff?

Why did my parents get divorced?
My mother's boyfriend is a louse.
He treats her like she's dirt.
I can't stand him being in our house.

My cat is psychic: she sends me
messages which I feel I must obey.
If it wasn't for her, I wouldn't have
even thought of running away.

I am always being bullied by other girls:
last week they locked me in the loo.
Because of this I truant school.
Please help me! What should I do?

The Body Shop

The day of the sale they all piled in,
the shop swarming with customers
all eager to find the right gear
to wear in the years ahead.

There were stunning outfits on offer,
the sort that would attract admiration.
It was tempting to choose by first
appearance only and some did.

The cheetah bounded out, chuffed
with his decorated trim physique,
as did the zebra and giraffe.
Some went well over the top

and emerged in gaudy outfits
as peacock or bird of paradise.
Others selected more durable finish:
turtle, for instance, or elephant.

But on the whole petite was in vogue,
crowds clamouring for ant or flea.
And legs came in fashionable models:
octopus, spider or centipede.

The assistants were helpful,
suggesting that customers feel
the quality and recommending
the human form as the best buy.

But which? Something that would
look good in jeans and a T-shirt
or perhaps something more classy?
A hint of tropical with oriental eyes?

It was a perplexing business
for those who didn't enjoy shopping.
'Use a fitting room,' the salesgirl said.
'It will look better when it's on.'

Mural

Usha came to school and got us painting
our drab walls. Under her inspiration
creatures from nowhere were brought to life.
You didn't have to be talented, only willing.

The drab walls under her inspiration
evolved into a jungle of exotic birds.
You didn't have to be talented. Only willing
to have fun with brushes and spray cans.

Evolving this jungle of exotic birds
took us far beyond our fixed ideas of art
and fun. With brushes and spray cans,
new species of vegetation flowered.

Taken far beyond our fixed ideas of art
we broke the rules. Colours ran wild.
New species of vegetation flowered
spontaneously in the spaces of our minds.

We broke the rules. Colours ran wild
when Usha came to school and got us painting.
Spontaneously in the spaces of our minds
creatures from nowhere were brought to life.

Special Needs

That people shouldn't call him names –
   it drives him crazy.
That Mum takes him to the Wax Museum –
   his favourite place.
That he keeps his dog Fudge –
   even though she wets the carpet.
That bullies shouldn't pull his glasses off –
   he can't see without them.
That he can go to the circus again –
   the clowns do funny tricks with real fire.
That his brother doesn't hide and say Boo! –
   it makes him jump.
That other people don't go into his bedroom –
   they mess things up.
That his grandma gets well again –
   he loves having tea at her house on Sundays.
That he be allowed to go to school with Emma –
   her jokes make him happy.
That his friends come call for him –
   he doesn't like playing on his own.
That he goes horseriding every week –
   with boots, trousers and hat.
That he can play his music whenever he wants –
   not too loudly.
That Dad shouldn't belt him –
   it hurts and leaves red marks.

Wembley

The world belongs to those who own it,
my dad always said. And we owned the road:

my dad and Uncle Mick, his mate, Charles,
Whiskey and me. Its tarmac and pavements,

its gutters, lamp-posts and most of its length.
We ran the hundred metres and the hurdles,

threw the discus and the shot, played cricket
and tennis and football until light failed.

Loudly opposing us were the neighbours
and, on one occasion, the police, who sided

with the smashed streetlights. Whiskey
was our streaker: she raced brazenly

from one end of the road to the other, barking
for our attentions. We only ever moved aside

for cars, but our road was usually quiet
except for last August when Whiskey chased

the bloke who hooted – and was somersaulted
five metres into a wall. I ran indoors to avoid

seeing her splatted, but later Uncle Mick
chose me as his partner to defeat Brazil

and we notched up a famous victory
on our front gate. I let in a goal, though,

when Whiskey's lopsided ghost
bounded up to me and licked my hand.

Day of Doom: *Part 4*

Not Over Yet!

. . . continued from page 73 . . .

The Story So Far . . .

In order to free our school from an evil power,
the Leopard Lady and I have managed to fly
over the ocean and enter Quox Castle, but our
host has instructed his men that we must die.

Now Read On . . .

The guards use teeth to tear my flesh apart.
I struggle to brush them off, then put my hand
deep into the machine's pulsating heart.
I feel intense heat but manage to withstand

the searing pain just long enough to grab
the gem which produces psychotronic beams.
Quox cowers wretchedly in a corner of the lab.
In my palm the Ventura Crystal gleams.

'You're finished, Quox!' I say. 'Had your fun!'
I hurl the deadly crystal against the stone walls
and it shatters like a brilliant exploding sun.
Lord Quox covers his eyes, staggers, and falls

onto his apparatus. Slowly he is sucked
into the activator and dissolved in nothingness.
The Leopard Lady, watching him self-destruct,
rushes over to congratulate me on my success.

Back at school everything is as it was before.
Mrs Weir serves me sausages and beans
as if nothing happened. The teachers restore
law and order and re-establish old routines.

But one afternoon during a particularly dull
lesson, I feel something burning in my brain.
I hear a voice calling to me within my skull.
I try to concentrate, but there it is again.

It's Quox's voice! Oh no! As good as new!
'So, my dear Phantom, I'm afraid you bodged
the job of eliminating me. I'm talking to you
by means of a micro-implant lodged

within your cerebral cortex. Clever, hey?
I'm alive and well – and more than ready to rule
the world. This time there's no possible way
that you or Leopard Lady can save your school . . .'

. . . to be continued.

OTHER POETRY TITLES FROM
HODDER CHILDREN'S BOOKS